The Crypto Mining Mindset

A Beginner's Guide to Cryptocurrency Mining

By Martin Quest

Table Of Contents

Introduction

Before we proceed with the basic concepts of cryptocurrency mining, I would like to thank you all for showing an interest in downloading my book. I have always been fascinated with this modern-day financial system. I believe that anyone who has invested his/her time and money in this book is one part interested in this new form of encrypted exchange, one part skeptic, uncertain and dubious about this concept.

There is nothing wrong with showing doubt and being a little negative about something that we do not know. I know I was negative once. Terms like bitcoins, ICOs, blockchains, cryptocurrencies, whatnot – they are all new for us, and we have every right to know about their history, workability, advantages, and anything in between.

Thus, in this book, I am going to get you acquainted with cryptocurrency terminology, as well as give you a brief explanation of how it operates and pays an investor. Does it have any potential? Yes, it does, but certain aspects make it follow a discreet environment.

Firstly, let us understand how we can define Cryptocurrency.

A cryptocurrency is defined as an asset fabricated to operate as a way of exchange carried out digitally. It implements a protective technology known as cryptography, which regulates the generation of more credit units and monitors their transfer between parties.

Simply put, cryptocurrencies are a form of currency in the digital world that do not follow the rules and regulations of a centralized banking system. Transactions work through a decentralized database called blockchain, which we will examine in detail in later chapters.

Bitcoin, which emerged as the first cryptocurrency in 2009, has gained worldwide fame over the years. It was Satoshi Nakamoto, a pseudonym used by an individual or a group, who developed bitcoin as the first cryptocurrency. Also, they were the ones to fabricate the beginning of a blockchain database.

Since then, numerous decentralized cryptocurrencies have revamped the operations of the traditional financial system. Bitcoins and alternate cryptocurrencies (also known as altcoins) are already witnessing tremendous growth, making them a part of new technology in the financial world.

With the digital era evolving to new levels, bitcoins and other cryptocurrencies are likely to grow exponentially in the future. With benefits that offer multi-operational utility in the financial sectors, cryptocurrencies are developing an open system that will allow us to exchange credits in ways that no one thought possible.

Thus, it is even more significant that you learn about this digital phenomenon and familiarize yourself with how it works to secure your financial assets.

Chapter 1: History Of Bitcoin Mining

In simple terms, bitcoin mining is a method of calculating the value of cryptocurrency assets through a cryptographic process. These processes mine bitcoins in blocks, which are simply ledger files that permanently record all recent cryptocurrency transactions.

You should know that the size of the block decreases as the number of coins increase. Any block starts with 50 BTC (bitcoin currency symbol), and as the number of blocks reaches 210,000, it halves. This results in a recurrent halving of the rewards for an individual block. This process is performed so that the inflation rate is regulated. Otherwise, there would be an uncontrollable number of paper currencies printing every second.

This concept in itself is proof that mining is not a simple process. It needs investments in the form of power, time, and computations. Also, with an increase in the time of mining these coins, its comprehensive power also increases.

Another fact to note is that the speed of emerging bitcoins is inversely proportional and drops exponentially. Satoshi calculated the number to be approximately 21,000,000, which can never be exceeded. Let us explain this mathematically:

A block takes around 10 minutes to be mined. And a complete mining cycle halves every four years. So, it results in:

Six blocks per hour. Multiply it further by 24 (hours per day), 365 (days per year), and 4 (number of years in a blockchain cycle).

So, we get -> 6 x 24 x 365 x 4 = 210,240 ~ 210,000.

After every 210,000 the block size is halved, and each block has 50 bitcoins.

So, sum of all the sizes of block rewards becomes:

50 + 25 + 12.5 + 6.25 + 3.125 + ... = 100

So, total number of coins that can be mined:

210,000 x 100 = 21,000,000.

If we talk about it in economic terms, the currency is divisible infinitely. Thus, the accurate value of cryptocurrency coins can be ignored as long as we fix a limit, which is 21 million. No doubt there can be a time when the number of mined coins reaches 21 million, and there is no more profit left unless there is a way to redefine the computations and new regulations are determined. But, that can take a while. Let us learn why.

The annual consumption of energy for mining bitcoins has been estimated at 30TWh, which is equal to the stable energy of 114 megawatts for a whole year. Also, an individual transaction of a bitcoin can take up power used for providing energy to about 10 U.S. houses in one day. Indeed, we can see that the energy consumption expenses for mining bitcoins are high.

Also, if the expenses of the mined coins surpass the costs of equipment and electricity used for mining, the cost-effective and less competent equipment will no longer be needed for this industry. This activity is economically reasonable, as increasing in the mining activities will increase investment in challenging computations, which in itself becomes expensive. In fact, the difficulty in computations has escalated to some 210,000,000,000 times. Also, the overall mining capacity for computations has reached 1,500,000,000 hashes per second.

How It All Got Started

Cpu Mining

Bitcoin mining started with earlier servers that let users utilize personal CPUs for mining. The first block header hash (a secure linkage between previous and current block) was computed using a conventional CPU of a computer, the Intel Core i7 990x to be precise, which was efficient enough to calculate at 33 MH/s.

Gpu Mining And The Starting Of Mining Farms

As time went by, the cryptographic mining industry upgraded its processing system to graphics processing units (GPUs). These adapters were able to perform cryptographic computations at a much faster rate than CPUs. The higher models of GPUs were able to calculate at 675 MH/s. Moreover, it was deduced that the calculative abilities could be even faster if one combined the power of more than one GPU. This linking of GPUs to mine cryptocurrency is termed as a Mini Farm, which contained a RAM unit, a CPU, 5-6 potent GPU accelerators, and a motherboard.

Gate Arrays

No doubt the disadvantage in initial mining was the requirement of a very powerful system. To tackle this weak link in the mining farms, a technology called Field-programmable gate array, or FPGA, was introduced. An FPGA is an IC (integrated circuit) that is configurable by the designer or customer once it is manufactured.

FPGA miners were evaluated to be five times more efficient compared to GPU miners. Regarding hash period, an FPGA computation displayed efficiency levels of 25.2 GH/s. However, there was still the overwhelming costs incurred while using FPGA mining processes. GPU units were still less expensive and had a better resale value once exhausted.

ASIC Mining

After the advent of the mining farms, it was found that the previous methods became economically impractical, as they were not specifically designed to run mining computations. This is where application-specific circuit miners or ASIC miners came into existence, which only served the purpose of cryptographic mining. These miners are almost ten times more efficient in mining.

One of the leading designers of ASIC miners was Butterfly Labs, which started developing miners in 2012 on pre-orders for potential customers. One of their masterpieces is the SC Mini Rig, which has the computation energy of 1,500 GH/s.

As mining became more and more difficult, it was almost impossible to manage computations using mini-farms. Lack of resources ultimately led to the migration of the mining technology to data centers, which were highly efficient in their calculative power. True bitcoin mining farms are justified using such setups with massive data centers to support the activity.

Cloud Mining

While ASIC mining using data centers is running currently, there is a new method of mining, thanks to the emergence of cloud computing technology. We call it cloud mining, which implements cloud-driven services for mining cryptocurrency. The cloud was able to save costs on expensive tools and equipment, and electricity, so the technology was favorably included in the mining process. This solved many problems that data centers usually involve, yet it is not 100% financially efficient. Almost 80% of cloud mining services present today are frauds, and many mining services do not pay the revenue after investment. So, this type of mining service needs to be approached very cautiously.

Hack Mining

Another emerging mining concept is hack mining. This is carried out using smart devices owned by other users. This mining activity is carried out using a special malware software which hacks into a device without the user being aware of it. After penetrating the device, they discreetly mine using the hacked system. Many users purchase such shady services, which do not cost much.

As a lot of power is needed to mine a cryptocurrency coin, a hacker hacks multiple smart devices, and combines the power of the activity. This way, the owner of the smart device does not even notice any changes. A case in 2014 emerged, where an anonymous attacker exploited a limitation in the cloud servers of Synology to mine around $200,000 worth of Dogecoins. More cases emerged, targeting mobile devices in their millions to mine cryptocurrency since the existence of this concept.

Hack mining activities are usually successful as hackers can read the software codes better than the security teams of the manufacturers. They tend to locate the vulnerabilities in their systems and exploit them for their advantages. Therefore, beware, as you may never know that your computer system is also helping a miner get rich.

Chapter 2: How It Works

By now, you know that in approximately every 10 minutes, new batches of cryptocurrency coins are made, with an individual coin worth $8000+ at current value.

Before I proceed with explaining how it works, let me first make you understand how it does not work. Firstly, do not get the wrong idea that cryptocurrency mining involves using equipment to search through the depths of the internet to locate a digital ore that can be mined into bitcoins. There is no actual ore, and bitcoins are not about smelting or extracting that ore from the virtual world.

It has been called mining because the individuals who get new bitcoins earn it in small and finite quantities periodically, similar to gold. Thus, the process has been termed as mining, and you are already aware of the halving system of the bitcoin batch in an interval of every four years.

Now, to learn how it works, you should know that all bitcoin miners are doing is comprehensive bookkeeping. A huge public ledger contains all the records of the transactions carried out in the world of cryptocurrency until the present. Any transaction of bitcoins between two parties has to be recorded and accredited by the miners in the virtual ledger.

It is the miner's responsibility to monitor that the sender is transacting actual money for mining the bitcoin. Once the transfer of money is approved, the miners validate it in the ledger. Moreover, to make sure that potential attackers do not hack the ledger, the ledger is encrypted with very complex computations that are almost impossible to hack. This service of mining offers them bitcoins.

There is always a competition going on amongst miners, who look forward to approving their batch of transactions to complete the computations needed to encrypt the transactions in the public ledger. Every new batch results in a rewarding activity for the miners who completed the transaction.

However, the computation process is quite daunting. Specialized equipment with hi-tech processing units are responsible for computing and solving cryptographic problems.

It all does seem exhilarating, doesn't it? After all, the process of mining has generated a robust solution to a tough problem that every digital currency faces, which is double spending.

The Concept Of Double Spending

What Is Double Spending?

Double spending can be defined as an activity when an individual transacts more money than the required amount. Most currencies online face this issue. Traditional currencies keep check on such problems by paying real cash or acquiring the help of reputed third-party organizations like banks, credit card services, PayPal, etc., which all transact the amount and record the changes in the account balances based on the transactions.

However, bitcoin functions in an open digital world, where third-party organizations do not influence or monitor it. Its philosophy counters the traditional approach we witness in the financial world. Thus, if I say to you that I have 20 bitcoins with me, how will you come to know that I am not lying about it?

Thus, to keep everything in check, a public ledger was fabricated that records all the transactions. This public ledger is referred to as Block Chain. I will discuss it in detail in later chapters. This public ledger lets you trace all the bitcoin transactions right from the very first time they were recorded.

But bitcoin is a digital currency, and is not monitored by any intermediaries. This technology's philosophy counters the monitoring activities practiced by third party enterprises. So, if you say that you own 25 bitcoins, how will I trust that you are being honest or not? The solution is that public ledger with records of all transactions, known as the blockchain. (We will learn about it later.) There is no way you can lie about the number of coins in your possession, when this technology fabricates a way to trace every transaction right from the start.

Thus, for every bitcoin transaction, miners go through the ledger and check for malicious practices of double spending. If everything is found perfect, the transaction is validated and recorded in the public ledger. It sounds simple, but it is not.

A public ledger accompanies a few problems:

Privacy is the first issue. How can one make sure that the exchange of bitcoins retains transparency while not disclosing their identity?

The other problem is security. If we talk about a public ledger that is open for all, how is it possible to prevent people from using it for their capital exploitations?

Well, to answer these issues, first you should know that a bitcoin miner does not own an account in which to keep his/her bitcoins.

Now coming to privacy, the cryptocurrency ledger manages to overcome the issue of privacy by using a deceptive technique. This ledger functions as a record keeper for the transactions only. It does not keep a record of the bitcoin balance or account. This way, all user information remains discreet.

Let me explain how it works with an example:

Let us assume that Rick needs to transfer a bitcoin to Morty. To accomplish this, Morty will generate an address virtually so that Rick can transact money, including an encryption key, to that address. The process is similar to an account with a password. The only difference is that Morty (the receiver) will open a new virtual address and a key for every new transaction. It is not necessary to do so, but to keep everything secure it is recommended that the transaction is done like this.

Now, when Rick clicks the send button to transact the money to Morty, the transaction chances into an encrypted code containing the amount and Morty's virtual address. This transaction is also transferred to all bitcoin miners on the internet, which includes all computers running the software for mining. Once the miners figure out that the transaction is authentic, it gets validated and recorded to the ledger. Let us conclude that the ledger authenticated and recorded the transaction.

Now, let us assume that Morty wants to send one bitcoin to Jeremy. So, Jeremy validates a virtual address and an encryption key. Morty eventually transacts the bitcoin by using the key and address that Rick gave him, and sends it to Jeremy.

Just like before, the transaction is sent to all the miners for validation. The miners evaluate the transaction via a reference number that points to the previous transaction from Rick to Morty. This is to ensure that Morty did not make any other transactions after that, which we call Double Spending. After the transaction is authenticated, every miner sends and receives a message of validation from every other miner. Similarly, the transactions for Morty and Jeremy are also validated for track keeping in the ledger.

This is how transactions in the bitcoin world work. People transferring bitcoins (or bitcoin fractions) to one another. The ledger keeping track of the bitcoins, but not the people or their balances. As a user creates a new key and address every time, the ledger will not be able to identify him/her, his/her addresses, or the number of coins he/she possesses. Thus, we define it as a transaction record that moves from one anonymous user to another.

Now, moving towards a solution for security:

The primary step that bitcoin currency takes for securing the public ledger is decentralizing it. There is no sign of a master document or a large spreadsheet secured on a server. Instead, the public ledger is divided into chunks of blocks, which are hidden logs of transaction that contain bitcoins in batches. Plus, every new block accompanies a reference to its previous block. This way, a user can follow the reference links and locate the very first one, when Satoshi Nakamoto designed this whole concept and bitcoins were born.

We refer to this long chain of blocks as blockchain, which incorporates the public ledger for bitcoins. As mentioned in previous chapters, each new block takes 10 minutes to mine, expanding it into a long chain over time.

You should know that every miner of bitcoins possesses a copy of the complete blockchain on his/her computer. If the user/miner switches off his/her computer for some time and then powers it on once again, his/her computer sends a message to all other miners requesting they share all the blocks that were created during this period of inactivity. Therefore, there are no special privileges given to any particular miner or computer. Also, no specific miner keeps a record of all the updates related to the blockchain. The information is held in check by the numerous miners, publicly.

Factors That Influence Mining

As the activity of mining is intricate, it is prudent that you choose the right hardware. One has to keep in mind specific factors that affect the overall performance of a bitcoin mining process. Let us discuss each factor.

Hash Rate:

Hash rate can be defined as the number of calculations performed by the hardware in one second. This rate is of high significance, as the higher the hash rate number, the faster the calculations, which will close the block and reward you much quicker.

Miners keep a look-out for a particular output from the hash function. For the hash functions, the same output is generated for the same input, yet they have been fabricated to show erratic behavior. Thus, miners try several random inputs to find a particular output for the hash function. You should understand that the competition in mining is robust, so to obtain a reward, a miner needs to search through all the random inputs as fast as possible. Thus, a higher hash rate facilitates faster search output – thus increasing the probability of being rewarded.

To measure hash rates, we use the unit MH/s (megahashes per second), GH/s (gigahashes per second), and TH/s (terahashes per second). You may have already seen these units displayed above, but now you understand their importance. Furthermore, a hardware's hash rate is particularly fabricated for bitcoin mining, which can range from 336 MH/s to 14 million MH/s.

Consumption Of Energy:

The next factor of importance in bitcoin mining is the investment in power input. Powerful hardware that you are planning to use for computations is going to need a convenient supply of electricity (energy). Before proceeding, you will need to understand the energy consumption of the hardware in watts. Plus, you will have to calculate your electricity bill as per the predicted number of watts. This calculation will help you to anticipate whether your investment in mining bitcoins is less than the rewards you are going to earn or not.

Utilizing the consumption of energy and hash rate in numbers will help you figure out the number of hashes that you receive for each watt expended by your hardware. For achieving the numbers, you can divide the hash rate by the watts.

Here is an example:

Assume that the hash rate of your hardware is 4,000 MH/s with a requirement of 30 watts, so the consumption of energy will be 133,333 MH/s per watt. You can even use an electricity rate calculator online, or simply check your electricity bill to know the actual cost of your investment in the power supply for your hardware.

Hardware:

At one time, the concept of bitcoin was too good to be true. People from a multitude of regions and cultures were attracted to this financial technology that offered freedom. There was no role of a centralized network, which relaxed users. Now, they had the power to check their transactions through an autonomous system that did not function through corporations, tax authorities, banks, and other third-party organizations. There is no one to keep an eye on how one spent his/her own money.

Moreover, in the past few years, the value of bitcoin was not motivated by mere profit, but was admired due to the unique concept and philosophy it followed. Back then, computers were all that were needed to transact and calculate the exchange of bitcoins.

As technology advanced, miners found that better GPU processors were able to calculate and mine bitcoins at a faster rate. In fact, the results were almost 100 times more efficient than previously. Thus, mining hardware manufacturers came into existence, and they started designing hardware specifically for this purpose. This conclusively gave birth to the concept of cryptocurrency mining.

Nowadays, mining bitcoins has become quite profitable. Many are even paying their regular bills through the rewards generated using mining of bitcoins. The mining farms consist of graphic card processors and cooling units to keep the computation running continuously.

Apparently, a mining farm will require a vast supply of power, which is not usually available to individual miners. Thus, the big corporations invest in the energy utilization and virtually gather limitless resources to create mining farms. However, there is still a way for individual miners to make a profit. And that is by joining with other miners and combining their power. This is known as a mining pool.

Proof Of Work

You should also be familiar with the phenomenon 'proof of work' in the mining industry. A Proof of Work is a part of data that is quite time-consuming, costly and difficult to produce. It is needed for acknowledging particular needs. However, it has to be more streamlined to check whether it satisfies the specific requirements or not.

Production of a POW can be formulated randomly with reduced probability. Lowering the probability results in more chances of trial and error, which is essential to validate before generating a proof of work. Bitcoin uses a hash cash proof of work system, in particular.

The hash cash method used in bitcoin mining helps reduce spam emails, as the sender will have to provide a valid proof of work in the contents of the email, including the To address.

Any legit email can show the proof without any difficulties. On the contrary, spam emails will not be able to do so, as there is a need for computations for generating the proof.

In bitcoin system, the hash cash proof of work generates blocks. This proof of work is attached to an individual block's data so that it can be validated. Its difficulty is also regulated so that there is a limit on the generation of new blocks. Thus, each block generation takes roughly 10 minutes.

Moreover, as the probability is set at a low value, the success of a generation of proof of work becomes unpredictable, as there is little information about the particular computer that will be generating the successive block.

Also, there is a requirement for validating a block, which is based on a lower hash value than the present target. In other words, every block that generates consists of the hash value from the previous block. This results in the chain of blocks that together incorporate a lot of computational work to produce Proof of Work.

Furthermore, altering a block will require reworking on all the following blocks. This way the blockchain remains safe from being tampered with.

The Difficulty Of Bitcoin/Crypto Mining

What Is Mining Difficulty?

Mining difficulty is defined as the measure of how hard it is to locate a hash under a given target value during the POW (proof of work).

Why Is Mining A Bitcoin Block Difficult?

Mining a bitcoin block is difficult as accepting a block is only possible if its target is greater or equal in value to the SHA-256 hash of a block header.

In simple terms: Every block hash initiates with a specific cluster of zeros. With so many zeros, there is a very low probability of computation of a block hash. This results in many trials before generating a hash. For generating a new hash, the hash cash function used in bitcoin mining increases.

The Metrics Of Bitcoin Network Difficulty

This network difficulty in bitcoin mining is a comparison between the instance it takes to identify a difficult block and the easiest block. After every 2016 blocks, this measure is recalibrated to such a value that the 2016 blocks from the previous cycle would have emerged in two weeks' time if all miners were generating at the same difficulty. This way, each block generates every 10 minutes.

With more miners adding up, the block generation rate also increases. This will also raise the difficulty of a generation so that it can balance the increasing rate of block generation and push it back down. Furthermore, attempts to add fraud blocks by exploiters are straightaway declined by all miners in the bitcoin network, so it is futile.

The Reward For Block Discovery

On discovery of a block, the user gets a particular number of bitcoins as a reward. This reward is given to him/her after consent from all other miners in the network. At present, the reward compensation is set to 25 bitcoins, whose value will be halved after the generation of 210,000 blocks.

Also, the users who carried out the transaction also compensate the bitcoin miner with a certain amount. This compensation is given so that the miner can add the transaction to the block. Thus, as more bitcoin miners join, the value of bitcoin is likely to decay. Then, the compensation fees for adding a transaction is likely to be of high significance for generating an income through mining.

Chapter 3: What Is A Block Chain?

A blockchain functions as an open-source ledger where users record, control, and amend transactions. The blockchain is no different from other platforms, say for instance Wikipedia. Just as Wikipedia is an open source platform where a single publisher is not responsible for fabricating content, blockchain too does not give full power to just one miner.

However, as we move towards a deeper level, we find that Wikipedia is running on the internet through a client-server model of a network. Here, users are first provided with permissions to amend content in the website's pages that are all stored on an integrated server.

So, a user accessing the page on the website will be provided with an updated version of the original copy for any particular entry on Wikipedia. Also, the regulation of the whole database system stays with the administrators, who are granted permissions and access through the main authority at the center.

Wikipedia's system operates similarly to the databases of other centralized and secured systems like insurance companies, government, or banks. So, in such cases, there is a primary owner who has the authority to manage, protect, and access any update to the system against malicious activities.

However, the distribution system and the database involved with the blockchain technology are quite distinct. While Wikipedia's original copy is amended on the server, which is not visible to the users (clients), the blockchain offers updates independently. Every update to the system is done on the master copy, which is visible to all users.

This difference makes it very useful, as this method eliminates the requirement of third-party organizations for digital affiliation. However, we cannot consider blockchain technology as new.

On the contrary, it can be termed as a modern combination of innovation and proven methods. In other words, it came into existence because of three technologies: a protocol to incentivize, cryptography with an encrypted key, and the internet. And Satoshi figured out this concept and changed it into a billion-dollar industry.

Thus, the blockchain technology prevented centralizing the system as building and securing digital relationships is absolute. Here all digital transactions are supplied using a robust, elegant and straightforward network framework that works as a peer-to-peer system.

Building Digital Trust

Maintaining trust in the digital world is often linked to authorization and identification. In simple terms, people online would like to know whether the person on the other end identifies himself honestly and if he can complete the job he claims.

The blockchain system offers a secure tool of ownership that completes all necessary authentication criteria. The encryption key is enough to identify the authenticity of the owner. Thus, there is no need to share detailed personal information that would otherwise have created the opportunity for hackers to attack.

Nevertheless, the relationship cannot be only based on authentication. There is also a need for enough money, authorization, correct address, transaction type, etc., which all requires distribution to balance it out in the overall network. This distribution strategy decreases the chances of forming a centralized body that would otherwise promote failure and corruption.

Furthermore, the distributed network should commit to security and recordkeeping. So, any authorization of a transaction will result in permission from the entire spread-out network.

Authorization and authentication, when carried out like this, allows the relationships to generate without the need for expensive investments. In fact, modern-world entrepreneurs have risen to indications of this technology, which is influential, innovative, and inconceivable. The blockchain technology has evolved as the base for all transactions carried out in the digital world, where it is building stronger digital relationships.

Chapter 4: How To Get Started

Now, I hope that you understand the basic terms related to the cryptocurrency mining industry. It is time to learn the actual steps for starting with the process.

Firstly, one should know that mining bitcoins in the current climate would be too expensive. If you had initiated mining bitcoins in the year 2009, when it started, you could easily generate tons of dollars. But, it is also true that you could have lost plenty of money. I would not recommend beginners who are planning on starting small to invest in bitcoins. The level of maintenance expenses and investment needed, accompanied by the computational difficulty in the process, is not lucrative at standard-level hardware. Bitcoins are not more appealing to large-scale industries who have hundreds and thousands of dollars to spare in the process.

However, we do have alternative cryptocurrencies, like Feathercoins, Dogecoins, and Litecoins, that provide benefits at a much-budgeted level for beginners. Anyone interested in mining any of these altcoins can generate up to 10 dollars every day using the usual consumer-level mining hardware.

Here is how you set up a mining process for any of these coins.

Steps To Start Mining Altcoins

1. Set up a coin wallet, which is a private database, free to use. It is like a digital Piggy bank that is protected with a password to keep your earnings secure. It also stores the open network ledger used for recording the transactions.
2. A software package (usually free), which is usually made of open sources and pool mining regulatory platforms, like stratum and cgminer.
3. Online mining pool membership, where miners have built a community to combine their computers and increase their power, hence profits.
4. Authorization at some currency exchange online, where you can trade your earned coins for traditional cash.
5. Continuous and fast internet connection. At least 2 Mbps is needed.
6. An air-conditioned part of your home where the hardware will be set up.
7. A customized desktop created explicitly for mining. Your standard computer may not be used, as you will need to keep running the system for mining. Also, your laptop, handheld device, or gaming console will not be of any use as these units are not able to generate enough computations for earning profits.

8. A GPU unit or an ASIC chip, which is a processing device used for mining. It can cost from $90-$3000 for either of these two units.
9. A cooling fan to keep the mining system cool at all times. A lot of heat generates while mining, which is why a cooling device is needed for a successful mining process.
10. Staying updated with the technological changes in the mining industry is also a requirement. New techniques and amendments are continually happening in this industry, so you will have to be aware of them to be a successful miner.

Now, if you still want to dedicate your time to stepping into the big leagues and mine Bitcoins, then the following method will be of use to you.

Steps To Mining Bitcoins In Particular

Step 1: Buying Hardware

Currently, the best bitcoin mining hardware for miners is the ASIC mining hardware. These machines work at solid computational speeds while keeping the consumption of power lower than GPU or FPGA mining systems. Many reputed companies have already manufactured great ASIC rigs for users worldwide.

ASIC systems serve the sole purpose of solving bitcoin blocks. With the increase in the popularity of bitcoins, their price also inflates. This triggers the rise in price of the ASIC mining hardware. For maintaining balance of cryptocurrency generation, its difficulty in mining inflates. Thus, it becomes almost impossible to beat the system without a decent ASIC machine to support the process.

Also, the ASIC technology used for bitcoin mining is improving its productivity, efficiency, and speed with time, so that it can be considered the best hardware for mining.

Some popular mining hardware is AntMiner S5, AntMiner S7, AntMiner S9, Antminer U3, USB miners, VMC Platinum 6, BTC Garden AM-V1, Avalon 3, Avalon 6, Avalon 2, Asic Miner BE Prisma, and ASICMiner BE Tube.

Do note that current prices may vary, so have a look at each set of hardware before deciding which one to choose.

Step 2: Choosing A Bitcoin Mining Software

Now that you are aware of decent hardware for mining bitcoins, let us move on to the software.

What Is Mining Software?

Even though the mining hardware for bitcoins takes care of the real process for mining, mining software is also of high significance.

- For individual miners, the software does the work of linking the blockchain network to the miner.
- For pool miners, the software tends to link the individual miner to the pool of miners.
- However, for cloud miners, there is no need for software to mine.

The Significance Of Mining Software For Bitcoin

The primary work of mining software is to transfer the computed work of the mining hardware to the distributed network on the blockchain. It also receives back all the completed and validated work from the rest of the miners present on the blockchain network.

With bitcoin mining software, the input and output operations of the miner are all monitored. Also, the crypto-mining software displays the temperature, fan speed, hash rate, miner speed, and similar statistical values.

Bitcoin Wallet

I mentioned a cryptocurrency wallet in the previous sections of the chapter. Well, a bitcoin wallet also plays a significant role in keeping a check on transactions. Moreover, a miner will need to have a legit bitcoin wallet before moving on to the software part. It happens because the software will request a valid Bitcoin address to send and receive payouts and rewards. Once you download or generate a wallet, you will be able to create a Bitcoin address.

You can find many Bitcoin wallets available online. Here are a few wallets, if you are confused about which to choose.

- **BreadWallet**: A popular Bitcoin wallet for iOS users.
- **Mycelium**: Android users love this Bitcoin wallet.
- **Electrum**: This Bitcoin wallet is suitable for Linux, Windows, and Mac.
- **Ledger Nano S**: Simple and secure hardware wallet suitable for all platforms.

You may have noticed that the Ledge Nano S is specified as a hardware wallet. This particular wallet is the most secure type of Bitcoin wallet, and is suitable for miners who earn a considerable amount of money through the process of mining. We will learn about it later in this guide. Now, let us move on to more about the Bitcoin software.

Some Recommendations To Get You Started

Mining Software For Windows

1. Bitcoin Miner

This mining software is excellent for using on Windows 8.1 and Windows 10. It provides a user-friendly interface with quick-sharing, mining pool, and power saving features. It also offers a feature called profit reports, which will predict whether your mining process is going to be lucrative or not.

2. BTCMiner

This open source miner for bitcoins is popularly used for ZTEX USB-FPGA modules. Looking at its features, the BTCMiner boasts a frequency scaling mode that autonomously selects the most dynamic frequency for the hashes with the highest rate. Furthermore, it is a ready-to-use software where there is no need for a license. It also accompanies FPGA boards that support it through a USB interface for programming and communication.

3. CGMiner

Any miner comes across this software in the mining activity, as it is arguably the most common of all among miners. It has been designed using the original programming algorithms of CPU Miner. A few of its many features are:

- Support for CPU mining
- Support for multiple GPUs

- Self-detection protocol for finding new blocks, including a mini database
- Interface capabilities that are located remotely
- Regulated fan speed

4. BFGMiner

It resembles CGMiner in operations. However, unlike CGMiner, it has been built specially for ASIC rigs and not for GPUs. A few other features of this software are:

- Fan regulation
- Combined overclocking power
- ADL reordering device by PCI-based bus ID
- Free mining with LLVM Open Cl/ mesa

5. EasyMiner

This is a graphics user interface-based software that encases other software like BFGMiner and CGMiner to make it more efficient. It supports both stratum protocol for mining as well as getwork protocol for mining. Plus, it is efficient for both individual and pool-based mining. Its main features comprise of delivering excellent graphs for monitoring performance through simple visualizations, and it provides with miner configuration.

Mining Software For Linux OS

1. CGMiner

Just like for the Windows platform, CGMiner is a popular and standard mining software that most miners prefer to mine Bitcoins. CGMiner reflects the standards of the original programming algos used in CPU Miner. The features for this software are the same as the ones mentioned in the Windows platform section.

2. BFGMiner

See information about it in the Windows OS section.

3. EasyMiner

See features in the Windows mining software section.

Mining Software For The Mac OSX Platform

1. RPC Miner

RPC Miner shows feasible compatibility with Mac OS of versions 10.6 or higher. It offers combination features with systems and APIs based on MAC OS.

2. Cash Out your Coins

This particular software will require a miner to cash out some Bitcoins to pay for the energy consumption, such as electricity.

Besides these, the Mac OS platform can run any of the software discussed in the previous platforms. So, you can read about them from previous sections. You can choose the software for beginning your mining activity by comparing their features and other requirements.

Step 3: Joining A "Mining Pool"

In previous chapters, I mentioned the term mining pools but never got the chance to elaborate upon them appropriately. Thus, let me explain the concept briefly.

Mining pools are parties created by miners to work and mine Bitcoins and other cryptocurrencies together. Thus, their combined power results in sharing the rewards based on the hash rate contributed by all miners. For an individual miner, it will be tough to find blocks, unless that particular miner is filthy rich to set up a super powerful mining farm. So, to increase the probability of finding blocks, miners mine together to achieve results at a much faster rate.

So, your most feasible step to mine Bitcoins is by joining a mining pool.

How Are You Rewarded In A Mining Pool?

It depends on the speed of generating hash rates. Hash rates are directly proportional to the chances of finding a new block, which in turn will bring out better rewards. Do note that each mining pool website that you are planning to join will ask for a particular pooling fee. So, expect to pay that as well.

Which Countries Are Mining The Most Coins?

Bitcoin mining gives more weight to countries with cheap energy consumption, such as electricity. Apparently, this has led to the centralization of the mining industries to only 10 to 15 major mining companies, which have taken over a considerable amount of hash power present in the blockchain network.

As most of the companies are concentrated in a few countries, only these few countries mine and export Bitcoins. Here is an insight into the major ones:

China

China is the leading miner of most of the bitcoins, and hence acts as the major exporter of cryptocurrency coins as well. China owns many major pool-mining communities, which have been estimated to own around 60% of the hash power. This also means that 60% of newly mined Bitcoins come from China.

Georgia

Georgia is the residence of the famous bitcoin mining company, BitFury, which not only controls 15% of the mining activities but is also one of the biggest manufacturers of bitcoin chips and mining hardware.

Sweden

Sweden's Stockholm is where KnCMiner, one of the significant bitcoin mining players, has spread its roots. It contributes to 7.5% of the mining of bitcoins.

U.S.

21 Inc., located in the U.S., is a BTC mining company situated in California. The firm not only executes a considerable amount of mining activities but also produces and sells low-powered miners for bitcoin, which is a product of their 21 Bitcoin computer line. The majority of hash power generated from the 21 Bitcoin systems targets the mining pool owned by the company. Their mining power can contribute 3% of the total mining activities.

Rest Of The World

The companies mentioned above take care of 80% of the bitcoin mining processes. The remaining 20% is spread out around the rest of the countries.

China's Mining Pool Concentration

In later sections, I will discuss the best pool mining communities to join. But, before we proceed, you should know that China is the leading region for major pool mining activities. Also, most pool websites are in Chinese only. This may be a big issue, as the major part of centralization for mining is in this country.

This is possible because of the low electricity costs in its region, which has attracted more mining activity than any other country. Not to mention, China is the major manufacturing hub and can produce the hardware units needed for computations at a much lower price than other countries.

It's rumored that some Chinese power companies point their excess energy towards Bitcoin mining facilities so that no energy goes to waste. Currently, 20 mining pools stand out as the most famous ones. Out of these almost 81% of the hash rates from the mining pools are controlled by Chinese regions.

Top 10 Mining Pool Communities Active At Present

Now let me introduce you to the ten major mining pool communities.

1. Antpool

Located in China, Antpool is the most active pool mining platform, and is currently functioning under BitMain. Antpool mines around 25% of the blocks.

2. BTC.top

BTC.top is a mining pool community owned privately by its members. It is not accessible to common miners.

3. BTC.Com

BTC.com is publicly accessible to join for pool mining.

4. Bixin

Bixin is another Chinese pool-mining platform that is publicly available. However, you will need to speak Chinese here to interact with other miners.

5. BTCC

BTCC boasts itself as China's third-biggest exchange platform for Bitcoins. Its pool mining community currently handles about 7% of all available blocks.

6. F2pool

DiscusFish, also referred as F2Pool, is another Chinese platform for pool miners that has succeeded in finding around 5 to 6% of the blocks in just six months.

7. ViaBTC

ViaBTC is a new mining pool platform, which is focusing more on Chinese miners.

8. BW Pool

BW emerged in China in 2014. It has almost a 5% share of the block mining under its name.

9. Bitclub.Network

Bitclub Network is another platform that has shown results and is quite large. But, there have been rumors about it being malicious.

10. Slush

Slush Pool has been there since the beginning. It is a trusted platform for beginner miners. Despite being the first pool mining community, it only racks about 3% of the blocks.

Recommended Pool Mining Community For Beginners

While it feels natural to choose a mining pool platform that has a major share in the activity, it is not always best practice to do so. I recommend going to Slush Pool mining community, which has been present since the very start of the pool-mining project. Slush Pool is operated by Satoshi Labs

The Process Of Joining Slush Pool

Anyone can easily join Slush Pool. All you need to do is:

1. Sign up for an account.
2. Setup configuration for your preferred mining software so that it points the hash power produced by your hardware to the Slush Pool's mining platform.
3. Share the address details of your Bitcoin wallet, which will be provided with rewards and payouts.

List Of Urls Offered By Slush Pool

To be a member of the mining community at Slush, you will have to show your software the way to the regional URLs offered by the website. This way, you can enhance your mining profits.

Mainland China

stratum+tcp://cn.stratum.slushpool.com:3333 stratum+tcp://cn.stratum.slushpool.com:443

Usa (East):

stratum+tcp://us-east.stratum.slushpool.com:3333

Europe

stratum+tcp://eu.stratum.slushpool.com:3333

Singapore/Asia-Pacific:

stratum+tcp://sg.stratum.slushpool.com:3333

How Much Pooling Fees Does Slush Charge Its Miners?

Slush asks for pooling charge fees of 2% on all rewards and payouts. Slush Pool transparently organizes its mining pool community with its users. That is why it shares the transaction fees with individual miners on receipt of rewards.

Slush Pool's activities are executed under Satoshi Labs. The firm is also responsible for the creation of a hardware wallet for Bitcoins named Trezor.io, and also owns coinmap.org.

Step 4: Setting Up Your Bitcoin Wallet

By now you know that wallets are your encrypted storehouses that contain all the payouts and rewards. Now, we are going to look a little deeper into their types.

There are two types of cryptocurrency wallet, which are: Cold or offline wallets and Hot or online wallets. Let us learn how the two types vary from each other.

The most fundamental difference between the two is that the hot wallets are linked to the online world, while the cold wallets restrict that connection. Most miners use both types of wallet, which provide them with varying purposes.

Hot wallets are more like checking accounts that you use more often. On the other hand, a cold account is like a savings account for keeping all your digital assets safe. Miners usually keep a small amount of currency in the hot wallets for trading. And a significant amount of their digital money is stored safely in the cold wallets.

Now, you must be wondering about the security aspects of the two. Let us explore a little more deeply.

Why Do Miners Keep A Large Sum Of Their Bitcoins In Cold Wallets?

The answer to this is simple. This way the attackers will not be able to steal their digital assets, as there is no online connection to exploit the wallet.

Does That Mean Hot Wallets Are Not Safe?

For determining how secure a hot wallet is, one will have to study the reputation and behavior of the third parties and individuals who are connected to the hot wallet. Anything that is linked online is prone to hacking and attacks. So, miners usually prefer keeping a small amount in their hot wallets, as an attacker will not waste his/her resources just to get hold of a small amount.

Types Of Hot Wallets

Account-Based Hot Wallets

Accounts that are stored in the online asset exchange companies, such as Bittrex and Poloniex, are deemed as hot wallets as they record all the funds of a user in their servers and infrastructure. If an attacker hacks the Poloniex system and drains all the assets stored there, then your account is most likely to be affected by the attack as well, as Poloniex is holding your funds for you directly.

A Coinbase account is also a type of hot wallet. So, if Coinbase is attacked, you could lose your funds too. This is why many practices keeping a small number of their digital assets in Coinbase and similar hot wallets.

Using Coinbase to trade and exchange bitcoins is secure, as long as you immediately move the money out of the wallet once the trade is completed. Many have found Coinbase to be a secure platform for business. However, it still questions the ethics whether it is fully secure and worth risking storing huge sums of money in it. I would suggest using Coinbase if you are a beginner miner, as the firm offers a user-friendly app and website for users, especially in the U.S.

Software-Based Hot Wallets

There is another type of hot wallet, such as Exodus.io, which is software downloadable and installable on a computer. Another name in the software types of hot wallet is Dash QT wallet. In this wallet, Exodus does not practice storing the private keys of the miners on the servers. Thus, the miners control their own money. However, there is still a risk of getting phished, as your wallet is connected to the internet, which can be a medium for a potential hacker to attack your computer and gain access to it. Exodus wallets are fabricated to communicate with the various blockchains directly. It also acknowledges many digital cryptocurrencies, except bitcoins.

You can consider several factors when choosing a software wallet. Exodus has been a popular choice among many users because it is user-friendly and has been combined with Shapeshift. This combined feature lets users avoid migrating to an asset exchange division externally, such as Poloniex or Bittrex to facilitate trading. With Exodus, miners have the benefit of not leaving the unsecure system. It surely is a great wallet, but it still needs to update its features to make the hot wallet more secure for users.

Types Of Cold Wallets

Hardware Wallets

While there are many types of cold wallet, the main one that we will focus on is the hardware wallet. This wallet has a physical body that is not connected to the internet. However, it does have a plug-in feature that lets it connect to the internet when required.

These wallets are very secure, as whenever a transaction is made, the wallet asks for confirmation from the user by instructing him/her to press the button present on it. You can consider them hack-proof. These encrypted devices are great for storing large sums of assets.

Three popular hardware wallet brands that miners usually choose are: KeepKey, Ledger Nano S, and Trezor.io.

Each one of these hardware/cold wallets has its unique features. For instance, Trezor.io has an outstanding reputation, and it was designed at Satoshi Labs. Trezor provides exceptional customers service and supports a multitude of currencies, namely – Testnet, Dogecoin, Namecoin, Litecoin, ZCash, Ethereum Classic, Ethereum, Dash, and Bitcoin.

Step 5: Start Mining

By now, we have learned all the beginner-level stuff about Bitcoins and their terminology. Do note that there is much more to learn in this network of cryptocurrencies, but all the above information is enough to get you started.

Now that we know which devices, software, and other equipment are needed for mining, it is time to start the actual mining. This last step is where you will learn about ways to improve your knowledge and stay updated about bitcoin mining and news. This currency and all the rules surrounding it are quite volatile. They tend to change often. Therefore, you will have to try your best to stay as updated about new techniques, latest news, etc., as you can.

Even though Bitcoin has been considered a risky investment, you cannot deny that the interest in this digital currency is increasing every day. You read this book until now because you want to learn about it. You have probably already set up all the accounts and hardware to start with the mining procedure, but before you continue, you should know that keeping yourself updated with any new developments in the mining space is of high significance.

Staying Updated

So, as stated earlier, the last step is all about staying updated and mining according to what you learn from such updates. This is not as simple as it may seem. You will have to dig deep into the layers of the cryptocurrency world to find information of importance to you in your mining activity. This can be very time consuming, especially when you do not know where to start.

Fortunately, this book gives you tips on how to proceed with the research work. So, let us continue.

Learning Through Widgets

My Bitcoins Gadget (For Windows)

With this widget's aid, you will get to know the number of coins you possess, their current worth, and it also lets you link to your pool mining community to reveal data and rewards, if any. Domchi, a member of BitcoinTalk, developed this widget. A new update has also been released for this widget after the previous update Mt.Gox collapsed. At first glance, the website may look malicious, but many BitcoinTalk administrators have already tested it and found that it is clean, simple, and safe to use.

Bitcoin Ticker (For Mac)

For MacBook users, the Bitcoin Ticker performs quite efficiently. This widget stays at the top of the screen on your Mac OSX and displays the prices of up to seven types of cryptocurrency exchange.

Learning From Internet Browsing Websites

Here are some popular news websites, which offer Bitcoin news and updates regularly.

Coindesk

This cryptocurrency-related news website stays up-to-date about anything related to Bitcoins and the cryptocurrency industry. A number of articles are published every day which talk about more than just recent updates. Many long-form pieces present on this website are worth reading, as they teach a lot about the world of cryptocurrency, its future, tips to improve mining, etc. Coindesk is also a great place for beginner miners to start. Their Blockchain 101 has been listed as a great article for newbies. Here, the most commonly asked questions related to the Bitcoin world are answered. Besides the cryptocurrency section, readers can also go through their other sections, which are Data, Research, Business, Markets, and Technology.

Cointelegraph

This site is an independent news platform targetting applications related to decentralization, the blockchain network, and cryptocurrency. It started in 2013 but has since garnered a massive audience, making it stand out as the second most visited bitcoin news website. Cointelegraph publishes a mixture of cryptocurrency-based commentary, market data & analysis, expert opinion, and breaking news. Cointelegraph also provides a user-friendly ICO calendar that gives all updates related to the launch of potential new coins.

Bitcoin Magazine

This magazine is more focused on Bitcoin in particular. The other cryptocurrency coins are occasionally covered, but a significant part of the website focuses on news updates related to the first cryptocurrency. This website consists of articles that are divided into five broader classes, which are: Technical, Opinion, Price & Data, Guides, and News. Each class further divides into subclasses that provide various topics of interest. So, there is plenty of information on this website, despite its coverage limited to just Bitcoin. It started in the year 2012 and publishes four articles every day, currently.

TheMerkle

This website is considered to be the youngest of all the websites on this list, as it was launched in 2014. The site covers the whole cryptocurrency sector, but there is an occasional turn towards news and reports related to other markets as well. Besides the usual categories of news, you may also find its review section educational. TheMerkle studies the finest cryptocurrency wallets and exchanges and reviews them. The site also provides comparisons on various virtual currencies and other financial equipment of importance. For instance, one of their comparison articles talked about the difference between stock-driven IPO and crypto-driven ICO. This site updates with up to 15 articles every day.

CryptoCoinsNews

CCN is a sister website of Hacked, but while the latter targets advice on trading and analyzing coins, the former is all about providing news coverage. The significant currencies covered in the news on the website are Ethereum, Litecoin, and Bitcoin. However, there are also updates related to other alternate coins from time to time as well. The site is more focused on a professional approach compared to the others on this list. For any reader who wants to study offerings of new products, changes in price, and mergers, then CCN is the place for you. CCN also offers an educational portal, just like CoinDesk. Though it may not be as detailed as CoinDesk's, it still provides vital information on the crypto sector.

Official Bitcoin Blog

This may be the official Bitcoin blog, but it only updates when there is a major announcement or news update regarding this currency. The Bitcoin team hardly updates a single post every couple of months, but when it releases, it gets aggregated coverage from all other news websites instantly. Nevertheless, if you are into Bitcoins, then you should definitely bookmark this website for updates. In addition, this is the only official platform that will offer you genuine updates about these digital coins. You can just add it to your current RSS feed and stay updated.

Bitcoin Talk

Bitcoin Talk is not really a conventional news website, but a forum, and a reputed one, at that. Over 1.5 million forum members actively operate on this website to cover and share the slightest update related to the cryptocurrency world. There is also a subclass for every possible section related to Bitcoins, such as trading updates, mining news, technical discussion, etc. A unique and helpful section that this website possesses is the Press Hits page, which offers one of the most broad-scale cluster of news articles for your knowledge. When you scroll down further on the website, you can also find a little section that dedicates itself to other cryptographic currencies and coins. Members share and discuss all major updates in that section.

Reddit

Anyone familiar with Reddit already understands the vast cluster of data available on it for educational, entertainment, and other significant purposes. Subreddits related to Bitcoins and the cryptocurrency industry are no different. You can find plenty of them available on the website, which you can join and stay informed. A few of them that will update all major and minor news related to the crypto sector are /r/CryptoCurrency, /r/Bitcoin, /r/CryptoMarkets, and /r/BitcoinMarkets. Do visit /r/Bitcoin if bitcoins are your number one mode of interest in this industry. Nevertheless, try subscribing to as many subreddits as you desire. You may never know when you get vital information from any of them.

Learn From Your Mobile Phones And Smart Devices

These mobile applications, which I am going to share below, are great at providing you with news updates and information on the run. Websites are most suitable when you are at your home computer or laptop. But apps provide you with a user-friendly layout that can be viewed whenever you get time. That said, here are a few popular mobile apps to get you updated with bitcoin information.

Bitcoin Checker (For Android)

With over 50,000 users and a rating of 4.7 by 3,400+ downloaders, Bitcoin Checkers offers you information related to the latest cryptocurrency prices. In addition, you can set alarms on this app that notify you about any major or trivial change in the cryptocurrency market, for which you can set up specific prerequisites. For instance, the app can notify you with an alarm when there is a rise or fall in the coin price by a certain amount.

Zeroblock (For Both iPhone And Android)

The ZeroBlock app not only keeps you updated on the real-time market prices, but also the latest news related to the world of digital currency. In addition, you also get a Bitcoin calculator incorporated in this application. This app has seen more user following among iPhone owners, who also use it for staying updated about current prices.

My Recommendations

No doubt, there are many portals from where you can gather bitcoin information at your convenience, but let us look at the ones that I recommend you to try out above all the rest.

WeUseCoins

WeUseCoins was one of the first portals I found very useful to polish my bitcoin knowledge. You are able to acquire news updates, starting guides, FAQs, Mining tips, and buying guides for bitcoins as well as altcoins. Some of the most influential bitcoin experts and miners share their experiences and tips on this website. In addition, you can certainly learn a lot from them. To get you started, you can read their posts about some of my favorite and 100%-noteworthy topics:

1. Decentralized Bitcoin
2. Tips on Securing Your Online Mining Presence
3. Why Wont Bitfinex/Tether Publish Already Existing Reports
4. Should You Buy Bitcoin with a Credit Card
5. How Latin American Growth Will Advance Through Bitcoin
6. The Process of Accepting Bitcoin Payments for your Business
7. BCash Hard Fork
8. A Guide to Claiming and Selling Bitcoin Forks
9. Top Cryptocurrencies Besides Bitcoin
10. Purchasing Litecoin

The Subreddit: /R/Bitcoin

I already mentioned it, but now I highly recommend that you follow this portal for all the latest updates regarding Bitcoins in specific. It is one of the highest-ranking platforms on Reddit, and this reputation makes it worth subscribing. You should note that other Redditors share external links here that will give you an idea of the most fascinating news leaks related to cryptocurrencies.

Coindesk

With an estimated visitor count of a few million every month, Coindesk is the largest and the leading source of Bitcoin information. A great thing I like about Coindesk is that there is no sponsored submission on this platform. This makes the posts more trustworthy to read. It may sometimes be hard for you to keep track of the number of posts updating on this website. A way to cope with that is by subscribing to their newsletter and reading the posts you find useful, while briefly glancing over the trivial ones.

DCMagnates

This website platform offered me not only the latest news about bitcoins and altcoins, but also advice and guides on trading in these coins. It has a great collection of articles comprising of news updates, trading assessments for Bitcoin, and other currencies, such as Litecoin. You should sign up to their newsletter to stay updated about any new posts.

Recommended Bitcoin Calculators

Some of the above websites and apps offer bitcoin calculators, but I found more useful information related to bitcoin trading analysis and calculations at the following portals.

BitcoinX

BitcoinX's profitability calculator provides the most extensive information based on the information you enter. The fields that it calculates and covers for your information are:

- Difficulty
- Mining Factor
- Average generation time for a block (solo)
- Hardware break even
- Net profit first time frame
- Coins per 24h at these conditions
- Power cost per 24h
- Revenue per day
- Less power costs
- System efficiency
- Mining Factor
- Average Mining Factor 100
- Power cost per time frame
- Revenue per time frame
- Less power costs

These fields are enough to give you an idea of whether you will make any profit from your status in the bitcoin world or not.

The Bitcoin Wisdom Calculator

This calculator offered by Bitcoin Wisdom not only updates the usual profitability information, but also targets the latest prices of interesting hardware related to bitcoins and other cryptocurrencies. It is worth visiting if you are planning on upgrading your equipment and want to find all competitive prices in one place.

Conclusion

Bitcoins have been helpful in reaping benefits that were never imaginable before. In fact, many major-scale industries are actually making millions by mining and exporting cryptocurrencies. Many people find these useful, because they have an international currency status. A person with bitcoins can use them in any part of the world by converting them into the conventional currency of that region. In addition, the security of the blockchain network is top-notch, which ensures that your money is sent to or received from the right person, and that too without the need of disclosing either one's identity online.

Many have seen the numerous benefits Bitcoins provide. A major one is that there is third-party influence, which would have charged a fee for a transaction otherwise. This is why Bitcoins are supported by many small and large-scale industries who do not have to rely on intermediaries any more. Support from users strengthens the existence of bitcoins, and if all people in the world start using it, then the day is not far off when Bitcoin replaces all currencies as the official one.

But, there are still disadvantages due to skeptics at the moment. Many hesitate to learn and become involved in it because it is an innovative and self-governing technology. But, with time, this issue can be resolved as more and more people embrace it.

Long Learning Curve, But Surely Worth It!

The concept of Bitcoin has a long learning curve that makes sure that the competitors are out of the picture. In addition, the rising value of bitcoins has been possible because there was very little saturation involved in this crypto currency exchange. With such a rising value, there is no doubt that many investment companies are promoting this cryptocurrency among the people to their fullest. Long-term investment in this currency will certainly garner enough assets.

The long learning curve may be complicated to grasp. But, this digital asset's performance is not influenced by individual companies, bonds/stocks, or the economy. No physical place is present that stocks these currencies in one place. And there is certainly no chance of hacking or exploiting anyone's assets (not that I know of), as the chain is spread throughout the internet. Here, everyone is an owner without any centralized banking system to control it.

Keeping the five steps you learnt above in mind will ensure that you reap maximum rewards by mining your favorite cryptocurrency. But, you need to invest in this field smartly. Being emotional will not mean that you earn more. Invest with a mindset that you may occasionally lose as well.

The Crypto world is like the Wild West, where you are free to explore, invest and earn as much as you like. You chose this book to learn about this independent world and found useful tips to get you started. My book will help you on the way, if you choose it to, but remember that the final decision to choose the right path is yours.

In the end, I would like to appreciate all my fellow readers that chose this book to learn about the concepts of Bitcoin and cryptocurrency mining. It may not have the advanced-level stuff, as it was meant to stay simple so that beginners can learn about it and move on to the next step.

I am glad you showed your interest in joining the new digital currency frontier, which has great potential in the future. Staying put before the calm will offer you a head-start, so that you know how to trade in the world of bitcoins and other cryptocurrencies.

About The Author

Martin Quest is an investor in the world of Bitcoin and cryptocurrency. Making every rookie mistake imaginable, he wants to help you mitigate some of the initial pitfalls of this brand-new world.

Disclaimer

References

https://www.investopedia.com/news/do-bitcoin-mining-energy-costs-influence-its-price/

https://www.coindesk.com/making-sense-bitcoins-halving/

http://forklog.net/bitcoin-mining-past-present-and-future/

https://cointelegraph.com/bitcoin-for-beginners/how-to-mine-bitcoin-everything-you-need-to-know#hardware-for-mining

https://www.bitcoinmining.com/what-is-proof-of-work/

https://www.bitcoinmining.com/what-is-bitcoin-mining-difficulty/#what-is

https://www.bitcoinmining.com/bitcoin-mining-hardware/

https://www.lifewire.com/cryptocoin-mining-for-beginners-2483064

https://www.coindesk.com/information/what-is-blockchain-technology/

https://www.buybitcoinworldwide.com/mining/software/

https://www.buybitcoinworldwide.com/mining/pools/#slush-pool-review

https://hackernoon.com/bitcoin-mining-understanding-mining-pools-and-increasing-daily-payouts-2b3b01eb87ba

https://medium.com/dash-for-newbies/cold-wallet-vs-hot-wallet-whats-the-difference-a00d872aa6b1

https://www.reddit.com/r/BitcoinMining/

https://www.makeuseof.com/tag/bitcoin-news-sites/

https://99bitcoins.com/8-ways-never-miss-crucial-update-bitcoin/

https://www.forbes.com/sites/forbescoachescouncil/2017/09/05/bitcoin-is-getting-easier-to-understand-and-its-pushing-up-prices/#1ebc910b2b1f

https://www.weusecoins.com/news/

http://www.bitcoinx.com/profit/

https://bitcoinwisdom.com/bitcoin/calculator